MONACO
PUTS ON THE GREEN

In tribute to Mic Chamblas-Ploton, who has recently passed away

The lightness of her pen and the poetic rhythm of her wording transcended Nature even as she fell under its spell.
Her precision and eye for detail gave expression to what I saw as a photographer.
Our many years of artistic collaboration will forever remain engraved in my memory and in my heart.
This book is dedicated to her.

Jean-Baptiste Leroux

Photographs by JEAN-BAPTISTE LEROUX

Text by MIC CHAMBLAS-PLOTON

Foreword by H.S.H. PRINCE ALBERT II OF MONACO

MONACO
PUTS ON THE GREEN

ABRAMS / NEW YORK

foreword

Palais de Monaco

July 2025

Gardens have always been the hidden soul of the Principality of Monaco. They are the expression of our commitment to beauty, nature and environmental conservation, in a region where land and sea are in constant dialogue.

This book captures the visual poetry of those gardens, beckoning you with superb photography by Jean-Baptiste Leroux. First you see my inner sanctum, the gardens of the Prince's Palace and the enchanting terraces of the Rocagel estate. These are the places where we take refuge — leafy embodiments of our traditions and respect for heritage.

The historic gardens come next: the Saint-Martin Gardens, the Exotic Garden, the Little Africa Gardens and the Boulingrins Gardens, all of them fashioned by past generations for the pleasure of those who came after. They bear witness to the generosity of our ancestors and a Principality that has moved with the times, bringing the past and present together through creative landscaping and openness to the world.

In addition to its heritage gardens, Monaco is also home to artistic gardens that serve as bridges between creativity and nature: the Princess Grace Rose Garden and the Japanese Garden. The first is a vibrant homage to the elegance and commitment of my mother; the second is a place of quiet contemplation where two cultures meet.

Then there are the green spaces of Fontvieille and Mareterra, two remarkable demonstrations of what can be achieved when urban planning shakes hands with nature. Created from land reclaimed from the sea, green spaces like these testify to our ability to find eco-friendly solutions of lasting benefit to us all.

As the seasons turn, Monaco's gardens reveal the melody of diversity.

May this book kindle a sense of discovery and wonder and, above all, encourage you to reflect on the vital importance of green spaces in our modern world.

1

2

contents

The Heritage Tree Trail takes you on an enchanting tour of Monaco. Planted with trees from the four corners of the earth, it invites you to discover the city tree by tree, traversing the globe while remaining within an area of just two square kilometres, of which nearly 500,000 m^2 is green space. From east to west, the trail passes through neighbourhoods and public gardens alike — a living pledge to end deforestation dating back to the birth of the trail in 2013. Extended since then, but always with a close eye on biodiversity, the trail today features 92 clearly labelled trees, each one assessed for biological, botanical and environmental compatibility by Monaco's Urban Planning Department and the Albert I Foundation. The result is a treasure trove of trees that is the envy of the world. All of them are showcased in these pages, with each one assigned a number that corresponds to a key on page 237.

3

The Palace Gardens

Rocagel

The Palace Gardens

Jewel of the Ramparts

This fortress was carved out of the Rock of Monaco in 1215, then conquered by François Grimaldi in 1297. By the seventeenth century it had come to resemble an Italianate palace but then fell foul of the French Revolution. It underwent a restoration in the late nineteenth century, followed by the addition of a new wing under Prince Rainier III.

"If these gardens look the way they do, it's thanks to my mother," says Prince Albert. "Originally, an orangery stood where the swimming pool is now, and the former aviary has made way for a teahouse. That was my idea; so too was the Asian-inspired garden with its bonsai trees and a beautiful Chinese table from my personal collection. The sculptures add an artistic dimension." Running along the top of the gardens, some 60 metres above the Rock, is a promenade planted with Aleppo pines that shields it from the view of passers-by below. A path to the side leads to the swimming pool with its soothing jacuzzi, fishpond and Japanese pagoda. The promenade itself terminates at the Rondeau, overlooking the areas set aside as nurseries for the office plants (foliage plants and orchids) currently being cultivated in greenhouses.

Beneath the ramparts stands the largest and probably the most fascinating tree in the entire Palace grounds: a ficus dating back almost two centuries (c. 1850).

A walk up to the Tour des Aigles follows a path flanked by mixed borders and ending with a table and Renaissance marble bench where Princess Grace loved to sit and read and gaze out over Port Hercule.

At the foot of the tower is a stone jardinière, planted with seven olive trees by her husband Prince Rainier III to celebrate the castle's seven-hundredth anniversary. Further up is a small rose garden and a statue of Prince Rainier by Daphné du Barry, overlooking the Fontvieille district that he himself had built. Everything about these gardens speaks of children's games, quiet dinners and discreet receptions for special guests.

A secret glimpse of the Palace Gardens Promenade, as seen from the port of Fontvieille, 60 metres below. Visible on the right is the new wing dating from the 1960s, with the tower rising up in the background; in the foreground stand the Aleppo pines that shield the promenade from view no matter how strong the wind.

View of the Fontvieille district from the Rondeau Tower, overlooking a terrace thick with greenery. Built by Prince Rainier III on reclaimed land, Fontvieille extends along the seafront and centres on this marina, bordered by apartment blocks and high-rise buildings.

Charming little paths meander through
a landscape of trees, art installations, parterres
and topiary, bathed in a chiaroscuro light
that is the genius of this garden.

The aerial roots of the *Ficus elastica*.
The longer its branches grow, the more
the tree sends down aerial roots for stability.
Originally from Asia, the *Ficus elastica*
has since won admirers worldwide.

A meditative Hercules peeks out from the foot of the Tour des Aigles, while overlooking the port, François-Xavier Lalanne's statue, *Tethered Donkey* (1988), and the pink blossoms of a sacred bamboo vie for attention with stunning views of sea and city. Pictured here is the private entrance of the New Wing — the latest addition to a garden where nature and culture await discovery.

Daphné du Barry's statue of Prince Rainier III (2007), as seen from the Fontvieille district that he himself had built. Perched at the southern end of the Rondeau, it has its back to the "family" rosarium and stands atop a flight of small terraces that run down to the Prince's zoological gardens. Further below are the greenhouses where the Palace gardeners cultivate foliage plants and orchids.

Planted with a wide variety of species, the Palace Gardens offer a "journey through history and across continents," to quote the chief gardener. Mediterranean and exotic plants come together for the sake of biodiversity and to keep the garden cool.

Sunrise on the Rondeau: Prince Rainier's statue, yellow forsythia and the children's multicoloured roses salute the day, gazing out over the silver sea and the awakening palace.

Rocagel

A return to nature

It was in 1957, a year after their marriage, that Prince Rainier III and Princess Grace fell for the charms of this old farmhouse in the uplands of the Principality. Nestling in 56 hectares of land, it would make the perfect retreat for their future family.

Tall cliffs offering breathtaking views of the Principality and the coastline from the Côte d'Azur to the Italian Riviera; meandering trails to other villages; lawns crossed by pathways that converge on a small chapel. Rocagel is a place where nature meets art, complete with two children's playhouses and animals that roam freely around the grounds. You enter to find a fitness area studded with holm oaks, firs and cypress trees. The residence itself stands at a distance: an elegant country house, set amid roses and fruit trees planted by Princess Grace, overlooking a cascading orchard of terraced cherry, apricot, apple, olive, fig and plum trees. Recent years have seen new plantings of olive trees to produce olive oil for use here and at the Palace, as an accompaniment to the vegetables grown in the adjoining kitchen garden and greenhouse: aubergines, tomatoes, leeks and aromatic herbs, according to the season. The eggs come from the hens you see milling about the property, along with ducks, cows, sheep and goats. "My mother was full of ideas and very hands-on. She loved roses but she always insisted on letting a bit of wild into the garden. I mainly take my lead from her, except for our historic properties of course." So says an ecologically minded Prince who feeds his soil with mulch made from the trimmed branches of the magnificent trees that line Rocagel's winding paths...

An ancient plum tree now sets the stage for a lawn and poplars, a sedate reminder of the bay laurel balls, acacias, Scots pines, old roses and spindle trees that once shared this site.

Pines and holm oaks, acacias, juniper and lime trees frame breathtaking views of the sea and coastline, bringing back memories of times past.

A terraced orchard plot planted with mirabelle plum trees, fig and almond trees, with lavender bushes and old roses yet to come.

4

The Saint-Martin Gardens

The Exotic Garden

The Little Africa Gardens

The Boulingrins Gardens

The Saint-Martin Gardens

An interplay of shadow and light

The Saint-Martin Gardens radiate the elegance of the historic heart of the Principality. Within easy reach are the Prince's Palace and the Oceanographic Museum; opposite stands the Romano-Byzantine Cathedral of our Lady Immaculate.

Planted on the south-western flank of the Rock of Monaco, the Saint-Martin Gardens rise up above shimmering waves barely glimpsed through trees busy with birds. To wander along these paths is to discover the untold delights of a Mediterranean garden created on a once-abandoned site by Prince Honoré V in 1816, to provide work for local people facing hardship in the aftermath of the French Revolution and the Empire.
The gardens today combine multicultural elegance with botanical know-how that successfully cultivates Mediterranean plants alongside acclimatised exotic species. The gardens begin where the Sainte-Barbe Gardens end, overlooked by the Place du Palais at the top of the Rock. The entrance to the gardens lies on the Principality's Heritage Tree Trail, featuring three trees that serve as an irresistible invitation to discover the rest of the walk: a wollemi pine, an *Oreopanax nymphaeifolius* (unmistakable for its lily-pad like leaves) and an Australian frangipani. There is also a tribute to the cactus and succulents garden near the Oceanographic Museum, created in 1895 by the Palace's Head Gardener, Augustin Gastaud, who was the inspiration behind Prince Albert I's Exotic Garden. Meandering paths punctuated with benches reveal a host of other delights: the waterfall quivering with koi carp; the seasonal celebrations of camelia, azalea and rhododendrons blossoms; and the iconic statues of the Chemin des sculptures Rainier III. Among them stands *La Princesse Grace*, by Livia Canestraro and Stefaan Depuydt, as seen in photos of every little girl who has ever visited the gardens. Perched on a bluff as you head back towards the Oceanographic Museum, is François Cogné's statue of Prince Albert I; off in the distance stands an insect hotel installed in 2019 to promote biodiversity. The path runs down to the sea, continuing all the way to an archaeological cave and the Fort Antoine open-air theatre.

Umbrella and Aleppo pines face the Mediterranean, creating a dappled canopy for rowan trees that celebrate the coolness with a touch of rouge.

Flanked by yuccas and Aleppo pines,
sun and sea put on a light show, watched by
a solitary, contemplative bird on a branch.

By the fountain, a stately aspidistra, also known as a cast-iron plant, brings a touch of colour to its shady surroundings.

Livia Canestraro and Stefaan Depuydt's statue of Princess Grace beckons from outside the garden.

Peer out from under this Aleppo pine and you get a view of the Fontvieille marina, dominated by the rocky promontory of the Tête du Chien, in the Alpes Maritimes.

The Barbary or Indian fig brings back memories of the much-travelled "navigator prince", Albert I, as commemorated by François Cogné's statue near the oceanographic museum as you leave the Saint-Martin Gardens.

A sun-loving euphorbia salutes the rising sun. Native to the Canary Islands, the euphorbia is heat and drought tolerant, and goes well with the Mediterranean varieties planted when the garden was first created.

As the morning sun plays with the trees
and waves, it creates a landscape quite unlike
any other.

The dialogue between sky and sea speaks to the poet inside us, echoed in olive trees that stand sentinel over yuccas and callistemons.

The Exotic Garden

A botanical journey through the tropics

Succulents were a passion for Augustin Gastaud, head gardener of the Saint-Martin Gardens. So much so that he grew them on a plot near the Oceanographic Museum, where they caught the eye of Prince Albert I. Monaco's Exotic Garden was to follow.

Finding the right location was no easy task — succulents are picky about their environment. Then, quite by chance, someone spotted a 'For Sale' sign, and the rest, as they say, is history. Perched 300 feet above sea level, the site forms part of the Révoires district, an area once known for its abundance of agaves and prickly pears and originally occupied by a small astronomical observatory. The land was accordingly purchased and in 1913 Monaco's Chief Engineer Louis Notari set about landscaping the site. The official opening came twenty years later, officiated by Prince Louis II, though works continued for another five years. What you have today is a garden studded with succulents from around the world — Mexico, South Africa, Central America, the United States — star-like plants that flower from spring to winter, opening at daybreak and closing at nightfall. A magical path in the lee of a retaining wall opens onto stunning views of the Principality and plants you didn't even know existed, some floral, some festooned around porticos and pergolas. Charming little walls and bridges, rest areas, walkways, vaults, balustrades, belvederes and colonnades — the rockery combines a wealth of practical yet decorative additions that reflect the heat of the sun back to the plants after sunset.

Some 10,500 species are to be found growing under glass at the Monaco Botanical Centre, located directly opposite the gardens, which exists to conserve, protect and propagate succulents. At the bottom of the garden, a cave unearthed in the former observatory is open to visitors — proof of a prehistoric human presence that is further confirmed at the nearby Museum of Anthropology.

Inviting paths lined with exotic encounters…
The garden is a meeting place for plants native to Mexico, the southwestern United States, Central and South America, southern and eastern Africa and the Arabian Peninsula.

Plants that bloom at different times of year create a mosaic of colours. Spring/summer sees the cacti come into flower, by day and sometimes by night, while aloes and crassulae flower in winter.

Opposite a blue candle cactus and a *Beaucarnea*, a crown-of-thorns displays its showy bracts; pictured on the right, a night-flowering Yucca rostrata offers its blooms to the sun.

Just a stone's throw from the garden,
the Botanical Centre houses one of the world's
finest collections of cacti and succulents:
more than 10,000 hot-house plants spread over
three floors.

Tucked amid a cabbage palm, a prickly pear and a desert rose, this secret path wends its way to a little terrace that offers a spectacular view over the sea and the different districts that make up the Rock — once seen never forgotten!

The Little Africa Gardens

A tropical forest in front of the Casino

In 1879, landscape architect and passionate botanist Édouard André was commissioned to design a garden that would offer winter residents the pleasures of spring and early summer in the coldest months of the year. And so were born the exotic gardens of La Petite Afrique.

Monaco's Little Africa Gardens stand opposite the Monte-Carlo Casino, alongside the Boulingrins Gardens. A rich array of exotic plants from the warmest places on earth share space with a soothing stream and cascading water features that tumble into a large pool. Visitors are free to wander along the paths and walkways, beginning with the Heritage Tree Trail at the entrance to the gardens where every one of the fifty-four specimens is labelled. Among these are a *Ginkgo biloba* or maidenhair tree, from China; a *Cryptomeria japonica* or Japanese cedar from the Far East; a *Jacaranda mimosifolia* or blue jacaranda, from South America; a *Wollemia nobilis* or Wollemi pine, and a *Brachychiton x hybridus* or Australian barrel tree, both from Australia; a *Metrosideros excelsa* or pōhutukawa, from New Zealand; and a *Pinus canariensis* or Canary Island pine. The trail continues along the Boulevard des Moulins, on the right, or, at the bottom of the gardens, connects with the Japanese Garden to the left of the casino.

The Little Africa Gardens are a place to learn and also a place simply to sit and enjoy the moment — park yourself on a bench and soak up the atmosphere, admiring the statues along the Chemin des sculptures Rainier III. At the top of the gardens is Andy Goldsworthy's slate pinecone sculpture, *Slate cone for Little Africa*. Next to the ornamental pool stands Claude Lalanne's *Le Dimétrodon*: a playful, water-spouting interpretation of a prehistoric creature that lived approximately 250 million years ago, its trellis framework festooned with plants and plainly very much at home here.

The cooling waters of the stream originally created by landscape architect Édouard André flow to this day, much to the delight of plants, birds and visitors alike.

The first tropical species planted by Édouard André came from the South Pacific and are still growing along the Heritage Tree Trail — an initiative that took root here, inspired by Prince Albert I

A white kurrajong, a queen palm
and a Mexican blue palm add their magic
to this garden path; pictured on the following
page is Claude Lalanne's *Dimetrodon* (1989).

This charming pool marks the completion of your stroll through the gardens. Unless, of course, you choose to retrace your steps to the Boulevard des Moulins and reacquaint yourself with the 58 heritage trees that embellish the garden and speak volumes about Prince Albert's admirable initiative and his Foundation.

The Boulingrins Gardens

Gracing the Casino

The name "Boulingrins" is a nod to the English "bowling green"; but the spirit of these gardens, with their formal layout, straight paths and ornamental pools, remains firmly French.

The meticulously manicured lawn forms a verdant foreground to the Monte-Carlo Casino, epitomizing the allure of these elegant gardens created in 1879 by famous landscape architect Édouard André. They were commissioned by Prince Charles III of Monaco in the days when wintering on the Riviera came with the promise of early spring. This leafy, winter-flowering garden fulfilled all expectations, featuring two walkways lined with exotic plants and a central area punctuated by streams, ornamental pools and flowerbeds. There could be no more elegant prelude to Charles Garnier's superb casino, managed by the Société des Bains de Mer, the group that operates Monte-Carlo's luxury hotels and leisure facilities. The turning point came in 1970 with the construction of an underground car park, dug out of the rock and capped with a concrete slab, followed in the years 2013–2018 by the arrival of a pop-up shopping parade. There was nothing for it but to redesign the Boulingrins and who better than landscape architect Michel Desvigne — the man with all the answers — to lead the project? In June 2019 the revamped Boulingrins Gardens reopened to the public, complete with a wide, lawned parterre flanked by trees and walkways; flowerbeds; three ornamental pools; and two sunken lawns alternating with three paved terraces. Modernised but with their identity intact, the gardens find an echo in Anish Kapoor's *Sky Mirror* sculpture: a fountain surrounded by palm trees on the Place du Casino, which is offered as a venue for public and private events alike.

Pictured on the previous page, a bust of Ballets Russes founder Serge de Diaghilev by Paul Belmondo (1973) stands beneath the palm trees at the top of Les Boulingrins. Visible here among the trees is the Monaco opera house and casino. The multi-coloured parterres in the foreground could almost be mistaken for ballet tutus...

The path ends by the sea, amid fragrant olive trees, a dwarf palm, a kumquat tree, dazzling flowerbeds and a lawned parterre — all the trappings of a garden that has reconnected with its history through modernisation. And Port Hercule, Monaco's oldest port, is just around the corner!

223

The Princess Grace Rose Garden

The Japanese Garden

The Princess Grace Rose Garden

A walk through colours and scents

This delightful rose garden in Fontvieille was established in 1984 by Prince Rainier III as a posthumous homage to his wife, Princess Grace. Enlarged since its foundation and renovated in 2014, it now covers almost twice the original area, planted to more than 8,000 rose bushes, representing some 300 different varieties.

To enter this rose garden is to enter an enchanting world of colours and scents. A place where you can wander at will amid 5,000 square metres of plantings encompassing more than 300 different varieties, the spirits lulled by the trickle of the bronze fountain in the centre of the garden. Set against a wall of water, it forms part of a centrepiece from which the entire garden unfolds before your eyes. Kees Verkade's impressive statue of Princess Grace stands next to the monogrammed wrought-iron gates that once served as the main entrance. As sunset approaches, the bronze effigy of the princess shines ever brighter, illuminating the "family" of roses at her feet: old rose and intensely scented for her; pink and cream for her marriage; deep red for Prince Rainier; creamy white for Caroline; coral pink for Stéphanie; and white edged with red for Albert II. As the accompanying labels make clear, each cultivar was specially created with a different member of the Grimaldi family in mind. Next come heritage and species roses dating back to the fourteenth century; roses awarded prizes for their exquisite fragrance; roses named after celebrities; prize-winning WFRS roses (World Federation of Rose Societies); landscaping shrub roses; plus climbers and ground-cover roses. There is a pergola festooned with creeper roses, and a parterre exclusively planted with roses entered in the Monaco International Rose Competition. Awarded Espace Végétal Écologique (EVE) certification, the garden is committed to ecofriendly practices — green growing methods, recycling garden waste, drip irrigation. Traditional, yet elegant and modern, the Princess Grace Rose Garden is all of these things and much, much more besides.

Kees Verkade's statue of Princess Grace (*La Princesse du Rocher*, 1983) stands in splendour in the garden created in her honour: a setting bathed in the myriad colours of wild roses and hybrid tea roses, overlooked by the rocky promontory of the Tête du Chien.

Shrub roses, climbing roses, standard roses – thousands of blooms planted in 467 rose beds prepare to unfurl their petals and release their fragrance. Covering 5,000 square metres of manicured grounds, the rosarium features a wall of water and a bronze fountain as its centrepiece.

The Japanese Garden

A journey through symbols

Created in 1994 by Japanese landscape architect Yasuo Beppu, this exceptional garden invites you to step into the world of Taoist philosophy — where every building, every plant and every water feature is imbued with symbolic meaning.

Yasuo Beppu, winner of the 1990 Osaka Flower Exhibition, first entered the orbit of the princely family at the International Bouquet Competition held under the auspices of the Garden Club established by Princess Grace. As a token of his admiration, Prince Rainier III commissioned Beppu to design a Japanese Garden, which opened to the public in 1994. It took Beppu two years to have the buildings custom-made in Japan; and to travel to sites in the Auvergne, the Tinée Valley and Corsica in search of the right stones, and trees adapted to the conditions in their new environment. Olive trees, Peruvian pepper trees, citrus trees, holm oaks, Scots pines, maples, camellias, Aleppo pines — the range is impressive. Depending on the trunk, some are pruned and trained Japanese-style, under guidance from Beppu who returns to Monaco every year to oversee proceedings. The garden's spiritual message is there from the start. There in the tiled roof over the entrance gate that keeps out evil spirits and brings a sense of peace.

There too in the teahouse, buildings, bridges, covered terraces, waterfalls, streams and ornamental pools, surrounded by *niwaki* and cloud-pruned trees and shrubs that add to the enchantment. At the top of the covered terrace stands the red bridge signifying the difficult transition to the afterlife, symbolized here by the crane and turtle islands of Taoist philosophy. The waterfall represents the birth of new life, the stream represents adulthood, and the pool is a metaphor for tranquillity in old age. The formal "Elixir of the Gods" tea ceremony held in the teahouse serves as a prelude to the nearby meditation space with its carefully raked gravel creating the illusion of ripples. Even the visitor information panels seem to exude a certain sagacity...

The covered terrace, or pavilion of contemplation, is an invitation to immerse yourself in colour, take in the variety of spaces and trees and admire a meticulously manicured landscape where everything is calculated to express an ideal.

Surrounded by striking plants, birds glide freely from one water feature to another — from the stream, representing adulthood, to the tranquil pool that symbolises old age.

Trees are measured before planting to ensure they are not too tall. Mediterranean species were adapted to suit the site and include olive trees, false pepper trees, citrus trees and holm oaks. Next came Scots pines, maples and camellias.

"The covered terrace, teahouse, red bridge and bamboo fences were custom-made in Japan. The buildings had to be made from a particular variety of cypress, using traditional methods," said landscape architect Yasuo Beppu. Thus did a Monegasque garden pay respect to its roots.

Fontvieille

Mareterra

Fontvieille

A district reclaimed from the sea

Fontvieille, like Mareterra, is a coastal extension built on reclaimed land: 32 hectares in all, conceived by Prince Rainier III and built in the period 1966–1973 under the supervision of architect Manfredi Nicoletti. A fusion of nature and culture, Fontvieille bears the seal of a Grimaldi widely known as the "Builder Prince".

Church, buildings, shopping centre, stadium — Fontvieille is a showcase of urban planning, and a testament to the vision of Prince Rainier III. This is a place to soak up culture, stroll among greenery, do business or simply enjoy life — dine out at the marina on the waterfront; take off from the heliport for an aerial view of Monaco; or breathe in the fragrances of the Princess Grace Rose Garden. Animal lovers can visit the Jardin Animalier sanctuary for abandoned animals; culture lovers can wander among the statues lining the UNESCO Garden on the Chemin des sculptures Rainier III — among them, César's *Le Poing*. The UNESCO Garden puts the finishing touch to a city space that feels more like an open-air museum, where people come to eat and relax among the foliage, surrounded by ornamental pools and flowerbeds. By the sea, a large marquee reserved for the circus arts and festivals stands amid Mediterranean and exotic plants that mark the beginning of the landscaped gardens: four hectares of winding paths, punctuated by pools rippling with carp where ducks and geese rub shoulders. Children particularly love the play area and educational vegetable garden. The paths twist and turn all the way to a lake, planted with Mediterranean trees – olive, pine and cypress – alongside exotic specimens like Bird of Paradise flowers, Firewheel and Monkey Puzzle trees (*Strelitzia*, *Stenocarpus*, *Araucaria*). Sculptures such as Pierre-Auguste Renoir and Richard Guino's *La Grande Laveuse* complete the picture, leaving you with the impression of an outdoor theatre on which the curtain never falls.

Brightly coloured clivias thrive in the shade, while elsewhere sun-loving strelitzias offer their petals to the light.

Pools and waterfalls framed by lush greenery create a cool space for pedestrians and attract birds — walking through the city feels like walking through a forest.

A leafy path beckons towards an inner adventure, beyond the world. Who knows what this Canary Island Ivy might have to say?

Mareterra

A green waterfront

Built on reclaimed land, Monaco's new Mareterra district extends the Principality's area by six hectares. The development includes 110 apartments, ten villas and four townhouses, all designed by architects Renzo Piano and Denis Valode. Greening the site was the work of landscape architect Michel Desvigne, with the accent on a Mediterranean environment from the start of construction in 2018.

In 2013 someone had the idea for a development that would satisfy public concern about biodiversity and deforestation. So was born the Mareterra project: a new, six-hectare waterfront district, opened in 2024, planted with 800 trees and 35,000 plants, not forgetting nesting boxes for tits and other birds. At least half of the area is given over to public use, featuring 9,400 square metres of green space and an impressive irrigation system that combines functionality with aesthetics: five pools in all, including a rainwater harvesting pool for drip irrigation, and a stormwater basin that limits run-off into the sea; fountains; and an irrigation canal that flows down from the manmade hill of La Colline to the Larvotto area on the shoreline. Adding to the enchantment is the reflecting pool surrounding Alexander Calder's monumental sculpture *Quatre Lances*, which stands in pride of place on the tree-lined Place Gabriella that connects with Avenue Mareterra. At the water's edge, the Grotte Bleue offers a view over the underwater structures designed to protect Monaco's new stretch of shoreline. Beyond its structural significance, the Grotte serves as a serene meditation area, its walls studded with quartz crystals that refract the light. The Promenade Prince Jacques takes you to the Larvotto, flanked by waves on one side and verdant walkways on the other. More discoveries await as you leave the Place Gabriella: climbing up the green slope of La Colline takes you to the Belvédère Gérard Brianti, named after the Monte Carlo rally driver, and from there to the Japanese garden with its brand-new pagoda. Alternatively, you can explore the landscaped gardens on the Colline itself: one hectare of gently undulating land between la Vallée de la Pinède and Avenue Mareterra, richly planted with trees and seasonal flowering shrubs. Mareterra – there is nowhere quite like it.

The Promenade Prince Jacques, flanked on one side by the sequined sea and on the other by reflections on still water — nature's superpowers expressed by water.

Mediterranean plantings are all around you,
gracing stone, soil and even water. Landscape
architect Michel Desvigne thought of everything.

8

9

Heritage Tree Trail

Pages 6–7
1 Carob tree / *Ceratonia siliqua* / Native to the Mediterranean basin, the Middle East and southern Europe.

Page 8
2 Cunningham's palm or piccabeen palm / *Archontophoenix cunninghamiana* / Native to eastern Australia.

Pages 10–11
3 Foreground: olive tree / *Olea europaea* / Native to Africa, Asia and Mediterranean Europe; Background: Peruvian pepper tree / *Schinus molle* / Native to South America.

Pages 88–89
4 Carob tree / *Ceratonia siliqua* / Native to the Mediterranean basin, the Middle East and southern Europe.

Pages 178–179
5 Weeping fig / *Ficus benjamina* / Native to Asia and Oceania.

Pages 210–211
6 Cunningham's palm or piccabeen palm / *Archontophoenix cunninghamiana* / Native to eastern Australia.

Pages 232–233
7 Olive tree / *Olea europaea* / Native to Africa, Asia and Mediterranean Europe.

Page 234
8 Port Jackson fig or rusty fig / *Ficus rubiginosa* / Native to eastern Australia.

Page 235
9 Broad-leaved bottle tree / *Brachychiton australis* / Native to eastern Australia.

Page 236
10 Cunningham's palm or piccabeen palm / *Archontophoenix cunninghamiana* / Native to eastern Australia.

Pages 238–239
11 Guadalupe cypress / *Cupressus guadalupensis* / Native to Guadalupe Island, Mexico.

Graphic design: Pierre Finot

Texts: Mic Chamblas-Ploton
Photography: Jean-Baptiste Leroux
Translation from the French: Florence Brutton

Director of Editorial Partnerships: Corinne Schmidt

10 9 8 7 6 5 4 3 2 1 Abrams books are available at special discounts when purchased in quantity for premiums and promotions as well as fundraising or educational use. Special editions can also be created to specification.

For details, contact specialsales@abramsbooks.com or the address below.
Abrams® is registered trademark of Harry N. Abrams

ABRAMS
The Art of Books

Printed and bound in October 2025 by Florjancic (Slovenia)
Legal deposit: October 2025
ISBN: 978-1-4197-9061-4

FSC MIX Paper | Supporting responsible forestry FSC® C106954